1

The Case of the Prosthetic Parishioner

"You Have Been Weighed in the Balances
and Found Wanting."

Written and Edited by
Pastor Chuck L Turner Sr.

Cover design by The Prophet X Commons

Acknowledgments

I dedicate this book to my mother Florence Lee Turner, the strongest woman I know. Also to my beautiful wife LaVenise Young Turner who has stood by my side through thick and thin. Also my children Cyndal M. Turner, the one who makes my heart smile, Chuck L. Turner Jr., and Devon A. Turner. I would also like to thank Pastor Sonny and Sister Julie Arguinzoni the founders of Victory Outreach International, one of the greatest ministries in the world, for their love, kindness, and example throughout the years. Special thanks to Pastor/Elder David Martinez (R.I.P.) and Sister Faith Martinez my spiritual mom and dad without whose help I wouldn't be who I am today. Also thank you to Pastor Augie Barajas and Sister

3

Mary Barajas for their influence in my life when I returned to California. Also thank you to my current Pastor Michael Gonzalez and his wife Sister Christina Gonzalez for not only encouraging me but allowing me to pursue what God has called me to do. And finally thank you to the many Pastors all over the world who have graciously allowed me the privilege of standing behind their pulpits to minister the word of God as I have treasured each and every opportunity!

Pastor Chuck L Turner Sr.

All scripture references are from the New King James Version of the bible.

Preface

This book is a prophetic word for the church today. To be perfectly honest the revelation has come as a result of my own struggles to maintain a consistently committed walk with God. I can say that for the most part over the past 31 years I've served the Lord, I have accomplished that goal. But certainly there have been seasons where my relationship with God has not been as vibrant and fruitful as I would have liked it to be. The Case of the Prosthetic Parishioner examines how the enemy uses subtle tactics to cause a believer to regress while having the feeling of progress. The word Prosthetic basically means an artificial limb, while the word Parishioner refers to a member of a church or congregation. In I Corinthians 12 the bible teaches that we are all members of the body of Christ. I believe that some Christians as a result of disobedience or sin have become like a prosthetic limb on the body of Christ. They appear to be normal functioning parts of the body but like a prosthetic they lack the full range of motion that belongs to a biological limb. They also lack the feeling of a biological limb, and like a prosthetic, no blood flows through them. The prophetic word God has given me will look at how a believer goes from being Beneficial, to being Superficial, to ultimately being Artificial, all because they stopped living Sacrificial. I'm convinced that this is a divine word from the Lord for the church as a whole. Too many Christians have forgotten that the word of God says in Deuteronomy 6:5, "You shall love the Lord your God with all your heart, with all your soul, and with all your strength." And have settled for an imitation version of what it means to live for God. So here it is church, The Case of the Prosthetic Parishioner! I pray that if you've begun to regress, this book will help put you back on the path of progress and fruitfulness in your relationship with God.

God's Charge against the Church

"The Prosthetic Limb"

I Corinthians 12:12-14 "For as the body is one and has many members, but all the members of that one body, being many, are one body, so also is Christ. For by one Spirit we were all baptized into one body – whether Jews or Greeks, whether slaves or free – and have all been made to drink into one Spirit. For in fact the body is not one member but many."

Verses 26-27 "And if one member suffers, all the members suffer with it; or if one member is honored, all the members rejoice with it. Now you are the body of Christ, and members individually."

Member – Greek *melos* meaning a limb or part of the body.

7

Prosthetic – denoting an artificial body part, such as a limb, a heart, or a breast implant. An artificial body part, a prosthesis.

Parishioner – an inhabitant of a parish, especially one who belongs to or attends a particular church.

Throughout my Christian experience, which has been around 31 years, I've faced many challenges and God has always caused things to work together for my good. (Romans 8:28) I can truly say that God has been good to me and that all the things I've encountered along the way have been good for me, although often I wasn't aware of it during the process. In listening to the voice of the Lord as well as the voices of the leaders of the church it has become clear that one of the greatest problems in the body of Christ is the believer who's not totally surrendered to the Lord and therefore not beneficial to the work. If we are members of the body as the scripture says, then the question becomes are we functioning as a biological limb, or a prosthetic limb?

I'm not in any way attempting to diminish the value of prosthetics in medical science. Millions of people are well served by the use of a prosthetic limb, whether it is an arm, a leg, a hand, or some other body part. When I reference a prosthetic I'm speaking spiritually, not physically. With that in mind let's examine some of the distinct differences between a biological limb and a prosthetic limb.

One of the things that stand out has to do with range of motion. While the person who uses a prosthetic or prosthesis will be able to perform many of the tasks related to their original body part, it can't replicate all the normal functions. For example, the leg may have the capacity to walk but not to run. It may not be able to duplicate the movement of the knee joint, or ankle, and thereby limiting what the person can and cannot do while using it. The arm may be able in some cases to carry something but be incapable of grabbing something. Because of design limitations and the complexity of the human hand, there may not be a prosthetic with that kind of ability. A prosthetic eye can be seen, but it cannot see. I think you get the picture (No pun intended).

When a believer regresses to this place those limitations hinder them in God's work. Much like a prosthetic, when they're clothed they look very much like the normal limb, but are exposed when performing a task. It's only when the person is given a responsibility within the church that their range of motion, or lack thereof, become clear. They desire to function at full capacity as they once did but spiritual negligence has cost them the ability operate as in times past (See Samson in Judges 16:20).

Some may say, "What about the individuals who compete in the Olympics or other sporting events with the use of a prosthetic? People like Oscar Pistorius, the South African runner. They're able to run with the artificial limb." It's true they do make a prosthesis that can be used for running, but I would imagine it's less effective for walking. So again, there are always limitations with an artificial limb.

Another distinct difference is the fact that a prosthetic has no feeling. Any limb, artificial or biological, if it doesn't receive blood-flow, it won't have any feeling. If because of some blockage my arm or leg ceases to have blood flowing into it, the immediate result would be numbness and then loss of feeling. Colossians 1:18 says, "And He is the head of the body, the church, who is the beginning, the firstborn from the dead, that in all things He may have pre-eminence." I would say that not only is Christ the head of the body but the heart as well. It's from the heart that blood is pumped throughout the body. When a believer is no longer feeling what God feels or being moved by the things that move God I believe something is blocking the flow of blood, (Jesus' blood) through their body. Perhaps that's why we sing "There is power, power, wonder working power, in the blood of the Lamb!" Or "I know it was the blood, I know it was the blood for me" Or "The blood that gives me strength from day to day, it will never lose its power!" I know we're not saved by feelings but you have to feel something! The only place where there's any feeling related to a prosthetic is with the flesh it's connected to. In other words that Christian is sensitive to their needs but probably no one else's. A Christian who has lost feeling will never answer the call of God for their life because they've become numb to the conviction of the Holy Spirit. No blood, no feeling! We all need the blood!

Also because the prosthesis has no feeling as far as receiving, it cannot transmit feelings either. You may ask "What does that mean?" Consider this, my biological hand can touch a person and transmit not just a physical touch, but emotion can be transferred through a single touch. If you're married, you can touch your spouse in such a way as to send an emotional message without saying a word. Our natural arms can embrace in such a manner that emotions flow through our bodies and communicate our feeling to the person on the receiving end. The prosthetic has no feeling and therefore cannot give what it doesn't possess. The "Prosthetic Parishioner" can become cold and callous to the needs of others.

It's in these thoughts that the Spirit of God is laying the groundwork for what He desires to say to the church (His body) today. We must all examine ourselves to ensure that we're doing everything within our power to remain a beneficial part of the body of Christ!

In the fifth chapter of the book of Daniel God speaks through the prophet to the Babylonian king Belshazzar. The 27th verse says to Belshazzar, TEKEL: "You have been weighed in the balances and found wanting." It sends the message of a judicial experience in which God determined he was not what he should have been. Or perhaps we could say he was found to be artificial. The ensuing judgement upon his life was that he lost everything, his position and his kingdom were taken from him and given to the Medes and Persians. If we have allowed ourselves to become a **Prosthetic Parishioner** then we will ultimately be weighed in the balances and found wanting. God help us so that our lives will be in balance before our God.

Chapter One
"Being Beneficial"
Walking in the Spirit

Beneficial – favorable or advantageous, resulting in good.

Galatians 5:16 (I say then: Walk in the Spirit and you shall not fulfill the lust of the flesh.)

I can remember when I was in high school getting my report cards and being happy to see I had a passing grade even though I had given very little effort during the semester. The idea of pursuing excellence or simply doing my best was non-existent. It didn't bother me at all to see a "D" on my report card, in fact in some cases I didn't mind if the grade were an "F". I figured as long as I have enough units to graduate on time it really held no significance. In addition to our regular grade we were also given a performance assessment remark which rated four categories: 1) Excellent 2) Satisfactory 3) Unsatisfactory 4) Achievement Below Apparent Ability. It was number four that I'd grown accustomed to seeing on my report cards. It's a remark that suggests a student has the ability to perform at a higher level but simply refuses to. In other words he or she, for whatever reason, will not give their best effort. Sadly, I must confess that was the story of my life for many years. And for some that mindset has found its way into their Christianity!

When it comes to serving the Lord, walking in the Spirit really has to do with giving your best effort to the things of God. Of course it means a lot more than just that but I believe that summarizes it pretty well. There are two things we need to effectively walk in the Spirit. First, we need knowledge of the things of the Spirit. And second, we need to apply that knowledge to our everyday lives. Neither of those things can be accomplished without maximum effort and attention to detail.

Here's the truth family and there's no way to get around it, **prayer and fasting** are two of the most important disciplines necessary to walking in the Spirit. Because these are Spiritual activities one must be in the Spirit to consistently practice them. When men and women of God embrace these as a regular part of their daily life, along with reading and studying God's word, they can expect to remain a beneficial part of Christ's body. I know that for many people the one thing I mentioned that doesn't sit well with you is fasting (although most Christians need some serious help with prayer also) because it is a difficult discipline to acquire. I'm not ignorant of the fact that there are individuals who have health issues that restrict their ability to go without food for extended periods of time and I would certainly not ask anyone to ignore their health. But truthfully there are those who exaggerate their condition because at the end of the day they just love to eat! Don't we all?

Fasting isn't just about eating or not eating, although in the bible fasting always involved denying one's food intake. It's also about spiritual discipline. It's about strengthening the inner-man in order to have more control over the outer-man. It's worth mentioning that it can help keep our focus on the things of God and not the things of the world.

In the book of Isaiah 58:6, God, through the prophet says, "Is this not the fast that I have chosen: to undo heavy burdens, to let the oppressed go free, and that you break every yoke?" It's clear to see throughout the scriptures that there are many spiritual benefits associated with fasting. Many people in churches today are silently battling with sin and incapable of breaking free because they're attempting to do it in their own strength. There are some situations where even prayer can seem ineffective when it's not accompanied with fasting. The person who's caught in the web of sin cannot be completely beneficial to the body of Christ or perform at full capacity in His work.

The person who suffers in silence is often trapped in sin and because of guilt and shame they're unable to seek help. The devil will use guilt and shame to keep a person in bondage. The fear of being judged or rejected by others can keep people from opening up about their struggles. The fear of allowing someone else to see our weaknesses can also keep people bound. The enemy will always seek to have us believe that we're the only ones who struggle the way we do and that we don't measure up to other people in the church. And so we compare ourselves to others and in our minds we come up short. I Corinthians 10:12 says, "For we dare not class ourselves or compare ourselves with those who commend themselves. But they, measuring themselves by themselves, and comparing themselves among themselves, are not wise." I heard someone once say that we compare ourselves, who we know everything about, to others who we know almost nothing about, so it's an unwise practice to say the least! I will say this, the best way to get free from sin is to talk to someone you trust and have them pray with you and for you, and also hold you accountable to make the necessary changes in your life. When you open up and let go of the guilt and shame you disarm the devil in that area of your life!

In the gospel of Mark 9:14-29, we are told of the account in which Jesus heals a man's son after the disciples proved incapable of doing so. The incident takes place following the Transfiguration of Jesus on the mountain in the presence of Peter, James and John. Upon returning from the mountain top he encounters the disciples disputing with the scribes. The dispute centered on the fact that a man had brought his son to have a mute spirit cast out of him but Jesus' disciples could not accomplish the task. Verse 18 says, "And wherever it seizes him, it throws him down; he foams at the mouth, gnashes his teeth, and becomes rigid. So I spoke to Your disciples, that they should cast it out, but they could not." Here's what I see. This man comes looking for Jesus, when he finds out that Jesus isn't there he looks to His disciples to cast out the spirit. After all, they are the disciples' of Christ, it's logical to expect that they could do the things their master does. It's really not a stretch to believe that a disciple would be able to do the things his master does. In fact they are under His tutelage for that specific purpose, to learn how to imitate His lifestyle and His practices or abilities.

Where this account really ministers to me is in verses 23-24 when it says, "Jesus said to him, 'If you can believe, all things are possible to him who believes.' Immediately the father of the child cried out and said with tears, 'Lord I believe; help my unbelief!'" This is an interesting statement, "help my unbelief!" It seems to me that he believed until the disciples failed to deliver the result he was seeking. Is it possible that we could damage someone's faith by not being fully functional as a Christian? I say yes it is! After Jesus cast the spirit out of the boy his disciples came to Him and asked in verse 28, "Why could we not cast it out?" Verse 29 says, "So He said to them, 'This kind can come out by nothing but prayer and fasting.'" If you read the NIV version or one of several other versions of the bible, you won't find this verse and therefore you may prefer to ignore its validity. But I can testify from personal experience that some burdens can only be lifted through prayer and fasting! Some people are only freed from oppression through prayer and fasting! Some yokes are only broken through prayer and fasting!

Clearly there are some spiritual advantages to having fasting as a part of your life on a regular basis. It appears that without prayer and fasting the disciples had a limited range of motion so to speak. They didn't at that time possess the kind of power they would ultimately receive after the crucifixion and resurrection of Christ! If that were true for the disciples then, how much more is it a necessary truth for us to embrace today? I want to be the kind of Christian who can operate with a full range of motion in the things of God so I can help someone's belief, not feed their unbelief! So I believe it's safe to say that in order to remain beneficial to the body of Christ and walk in the Spirit, we must include prayer and fasting as a key ingredient to our lives as Christians.

Another quality we need to consider as we strive to walk in the Spirit is **obedience**. In this age of Post-Modernism and Political-Correctness, along with several other variations of New Age thinking, obedience has become an increasingly unpopular subject. Especially within the church, where obedience, along with commitment, have become sore subjects for a lot of pastors. Let's face it, obedience is not in our nature, it requires the work of the Holy Spirit. The reason I say that is because true obedience for the Christian comes as a result of submission which is matter of the heart. I can remember as a baby Christian hearing certain people compare our obedience to that of an animal obeying his master or trainer. The truth is that's a terrible analogy. An animal's obedience is not necessarily born out of love. It is in most cases simply learned behavior. There's usually some type of reward used to train an animal to obey a given command because without the reward there would be no behavior. But we know and understand that God is not simply looking for learned behavior, He's looking for the type of obedience that comes as a believer lives his/her life in total submission to His will.

Let me first say that I often struggle with obedience as much as the next person. So I'm not sitting on my high horse looking down on the world and scolding everyone for not being like me. In fact I realize that in the future there will be challenges that will test my willingness to obey and these words I've written will hit me like a ton of bricks. But the fact that it's a struggle for me makes it no less of a truth. If we're honest with ourselves we would admit that this is an area of difficulty for us all. The bible says in Hebrews 13:17, "Obey those who rule over you, and be submissive, for they watch out for your souls, as those who must give account. Let them do so with joy and not with grief, for that would be unprofitable for you." Notice the words "and be submissive," this clearly makes the point that it isn't just about the action but the motive behind the action. The word submissive or submit comes from the Greek words *hupo (hoop-o)* meaning to place under or beneath, and *hupeiko (hoop-i-ko)* meaning to yield, be "weak", or to surrender. Show me the person who claims to have mastered that verse, and I'll show you a liar!

Let's re-visit the words "and be submissive" and consider the implications of that thought as we evaluate our own obedience to God and the leadership we serve under. Remember we're talking about being beneficial to the body of Christ and operating with a full range of motion as part of the body. With that in mind we must accept the fact that every area of disobedience demonstrates a limited range of motion as a part of the body and therefore reflects the characteristic of a prosthetic limb. We all desire to love the

Lord our God with all our heart, with all our soul, and with all our strength. ("The Shema" Deuteronomy 6:5) We also want to worship God in spirit and truth. (John 4:24) But sadly, there are times when quite frankly, that just isn't the case. We frequently fail to honor those verses and we begrudgingly obey the Lord or those He's placed over our lives. It is because of challenges like this that prayer and fasting become so important to our relationship with God. With our outer-man warring against our inner-man, it's only through the power of the Holy Spirit that we can be victorious! As I stated earlier, it's only with great effort in the spiritual things and much attention to detail that we can remain as beneficial to the body of Christ as God intends for us to be. I confess that on many occasions I've been obedient mostly to maintain the outer appearance and not out of a submitted heart. And if you're like me, you have too.

So what does it take to walk in the Spirit through obedience? I don't presuppose to have all the answers but I do know it takes a revelation from God. The very real and present danger of disobedience must be revealed to us through the Holy Spirit in order for one to have an earnest desire to obey. I believe that people are not changed by information or explanation, but by the revelation of God's will for their lives. When a person is impacted by revelation it will manifest itself in their lives through application. When a child of God applies obedience to their life they position themselves for God's blessing. What I've experienced in my walk with God is that when truth is revealed to me through the work of the Holy Spirit it has resulted in an immediate desire to change. Jesus told the disciples in the Garden of Gethsemane to "Watch and pray, lest you enter into temptation. The spirit indeed is willing, but the flesh is weak" (Matt. 26:41) though it was spoken in reference to prayer, it can be applied the area of obedience in our Christian life. I say that because the disciples were asked to wait with Jesus and by sleeping they were found to be disobedient to that request. There is definitely a temptation to disobey, and that is because of the work of the flesh or outer-man. Romans 7:22 says, "For I delight in the law of God according to the inward man." The scripture clearly teaches that obedience is a desire of the spirit man or inner-man, and the spirit man is strengthened for obedience through the power of the Holy Spirit. This is why we need revelation from God to live an obedient life.

So having said that walking in the Spirit through obedience requires submission to leadership, and that only happens as a result of receiving a revelation from God. Let's turn our attention to another area of obedience that helps us remain beneficial to the body of Christ. We must have an **obedient tongue**. So much of what we say has a direct impact on our being beneficial to the body of Christ. Every Christian has the power to make faith and encouragement a regular part of their conversation but many people refuse to govern their tongue in order to be a blessing to the body. Admittedly this may be the most difficult area to maintain control over but it also may be the most important. The bible says in Proverbs 18:21, "Death and life are in the power of the tongue, and those who love it will eat its fruit." Obviously there are great advantages to speaking life into the various people and situations we face on a daily basis. We are taught through this scripture that our words influence the things we experience in life.

The person with an obedient tongue will utilize their speech to build others up and not to tear others down. Hebrews 10:24 says, "And let us consider one another in order to stir up love and good works," which is an indictment against those who use their words to gossip and criticize. In order to avoid this type of behavior it's important to remember God's commandment to "love your neighbor as yourself" which can be found in Matthew 19:19, with the thought taken from the Ten Commandments in Exodus 20:2-17. Anyone who practices speaking kindly to others in an effort to build up and encourage will be beneficial to the body. The ministry of encouragement can often help people to discover and walk in their God-given assignment and that is always a much needed gift in the church.

The believer who practices an obedient tongue will also speak the truth. In Proverbs 6:16-19 "a lying tongue" is included in the seven abominations. Unfortunately because of our sinful nature lying is a lot easier than we'd like it to be. Usually all it takes is for someone to ask a question we're either uncomfortable with or we're simply unprepared to answer and we can find ourselves being dishonest. In James 3:8 the bible says "But no man can tame the tongue" which gives great significance to the words of our parents when they told us "Watch your mouth!" Growing up, because of my propensity to use profanity, I heard that phrase quite often. Here's an illustration that I find helpful and perhaps you will too. I'm the type of person who upon visiting someone who owns a dog, particularly a large dog, one of my main concerns is whether or not the dog is tame. Of course most dog owners will always proclaim, "Oh no, he doesn't bite!" Maybe it's just me but most of the time the dog is communicating an entirely different message to me. My point is that because I'm not convinced the dog is tame I keep my eye on him if he's not confined to the back yard and allowed to roam freely through the house. So if I need to "watch" a dog, which may or may not be tame, I should

32

probably "watch" my tongue which the bible says cannot be tamed.

Also as we give our attention to speaking the truth it's necessary to consider that even the truth needs the proper motivation. Ephesians 4:15 teaches that we should "speak the truth in love", it's the words "in love" that give us the insight as to the inspiration behind speaking the truth. Let us not forget that the truth, when not spoken in love can be very damaging and hurtful. For instance speaking about someone's weight, clothing, marital/family issues, or personal struggles may not be acceptable even if it is true. When we're motivated by love we'll be very careful to make sure that the things we say are constructive, not destructive.

There are obviously many other things that can be said about **Walking in the Spirit** but suffice it to say that **Prayer and Fasting** along with **Obedience** is a great place to start! By giving our undivided attention to those areas many wonderful things will flow through our lives and into the lives of others. The men and women who are most beneficial to the body of Christ are actively pursuing their God given calling in life and operating with a full range of motion in the things of the Spirit. I believe the prophetic word of God to the church today is that we live our lives in the place where we are the most beneficial to the work He's called us to.

I would like to pause and clarify what I mean when I use the phrase "full range of motion" as it relates to the subject matter being discussed. The Christian who is beneficial to the body of Christ will be fully operational in every area of their spiritual life. For example, in love, in patience, in prayer and fasting, in servant-hood, in the ministry of helps, in hospitality, in giving, in faithfulness to the ministry they belong to, in the word of God, in their witness, and you can fill in the blank if you feel I've left anything out. In other words those who are beneficial members of the body are fully functional in the things of God!

Finally, I suppose it would be criminal for me to write about this subject and neglect to mention the fruit of the Spirit. At the risk of being redundant, (considering the previous paragraph) they are love, joy, peace, longsuffering, kindness, goodness, faithfulness, gentleness, and self-control, as listed in Galatians 5:22-23. I would personally include giving as a fruit of the Spirit as well, but that's another message entirely. Again I reiterate that if prayer, fasting and obedience are practiced consistently in the Christian life, the by-product will be the fruit of the Spirit! I speak to you under the inspiration of the Holy Spirit and exhort you to do all you can to remain a beneficial part of the body of Christ!

Chapter Two
"Being Superficial"
Self-Centeredness

Superficial – existing or occurring at or on the surface; appearing to be true, or real, only until examined more closely.

Luke 9:57-62:
57 Now it happened as they journeyed on the road, that someone said to Him, "Lord I will follow you wherever you go." 58 And Jesus said to him, "Foxes have holes and birds of the air have nests, but the Son of Man has nowhere to lay His head." 59 Then He said to another, "Follow Me." But he said, "Lord let me first go and bury my father." 60 Jesus said to him, "Let the dead bury their own dead, but you go and preach the kingdom of God." 61 And another also said, "Lord I will follow You, but let me first go and bid them farewell who are at my house." 62 But Jesus said to him, "No one,

having put his hand to the plow, and looking back, is fit for the kingdom of God."

The above passages teach about the cost of discipleship. What I see are three individuals who each possessed a superficial commitment and were therefore incapable of living up to God's standard for service. It appears that when they were challenged to enter into a relationship that required putting God's purposes above their own, they were less enthused about following. Being superficial is a very dangerous place to be because it can lead to becoming artificial, which we will discuss in the next chapter. My experience in ministry has been that many superficial believers were previously beneficial but over time they have regressed. One of the great deceptions of the enemy is to lure Christians from dependence on God, to independence from God while convincing them that they're still living the life He's called them to.

For the majority of Christians, the longer they're in church the less involved they become. It becomes easier for them to disassociate service in the ministry from serving God. The logic goes something like this, "I don't need to do all of those things anymore like I did when I was a new Christian. I really need to focus on myself and my family. Besides, I serve God, not the church." Somewhere along the way one can lose sight of the fact that our Christianity is not to be self-centered, but others-centered. The superficial believer is only superficial when it concerns others', he/she are totally committed to self. The devil wraps this lie in the disguise of maturity. Typically the person is convinced they're progressing when in fact they're regressing. The true or beneficial believer never abandons the practice of servant-hood, but recognizes it as the cornerstone of an active faith.

Let's examine another example of the superficial believer in the scriptures. In Luke 8:4-8 Jesus shares the Parable of the Sower. It reads like this: "And when a great multitude had gathered, and they had come to Him from every city, He spoke by a parable: 'A sower went out to sow his seed. And as he sowed, some fell by the wayside; and it was trampled down, and the birds of the air devoured it. Some fell on rock; and as soon as it sprung up, it withered away because it lacked moisture. And some fell among thorns, and the thorns sprang up with it and choked it. But others fell on good ground, sprang up, and yielded a crop a hundredfold.' When He had said these things He cried, 'He who has ears to hear, let him hear!'"

In the above passages we're given three examples of the superficial believer, and one example of the beneficial believer. If you're somewhat familiar with the bible you know that the seed is typology for the word of God, and the various soils described are typology for people and how they receive the word. In verses 11-15 He says that those by the wayside are the ones who are easily deceived by the devil and have the word taken away before they can believe and be saved. They're commitment is superficial because they don't value the word of God and are therefore easily susceptible to the lies of the enemy. Jesus goes on to explain that the seed on the rock are people who joyfully receive the word but don't last because of temptation. That's a superficial commitment made primarily on good feelings, which will never carry a person over the long haul. The ones that fell among thorns are those who are distracted by the cares, riches, and the pleasures of life. They're superficial because too many things matter more than God and He can never take His rightful place in their lives. And lastly there is the beneficial believer who receives the word and is productive with it and bears much fruit in his/her life.

What I believe God is speaking to His people about today is the danger of starting off as a productive and beneficial member of the body. But to over a period of time for a variety of reasons begin to regress and become unproductive and superficial. No longer striving to, "press toward the goal for the prize of the upward call of God in Christ Jesus." (Phil. 3:14) But now content to live an average Christian life that doesn't constitute giving our lives to Jesus in total surrender to His will. It is this very path that leads toward becoming the Prosthetic Parishioner! The one that maintains the outward appearance of a vibrant life, while being dead on the inside. Many Christians today have given in to this kind of lifestyle and as a result the body of Christ suffers.

Spiritual Numbness

Superficiality is the beginning stage of becoming a Prosthetic Parishioner. I'm convinced that God is speaking to the body of Christ and saying, "Beware of being a superficial part of the body because of where it can lead to!" It's an early warning sign similar to numbness being an early warning sign of a loss of feeling. The Lord revealed to me that spiritual numbness is the root cause of being superficial in our commitment to God. Numbness is not the total loss of feeling, but it is a condition that can evolve into total loss of feeling.

Let's take a look at what medical science says about numbness as stated by Medicine Plus Medical Encyclopedia: "Numbness and tingling are abnormal sensations that can occur anywhere in your body, but they are often felt in your fingers, hands, feet, arms, or legs. There are many possible causes of numbness and tingling, including... injuring a nerve." (May 15, 2017) Another statement from Healthline says it is usually "caused by a decrease in blood flow to the nerves."

The condition of spiritual numbness that leads to superficiality is also felt through a tingling sensation. That tingling is the result of the lies of the devil encouraging us to dial down our commitment to the things of God. It's those whispers in our spiritual ear saying we've reached a level of maturity where we don't need the kind of accountability we had early in our walk with Christ. When a person entertains those thoughts it can lead to distancing ones' self from the leadership God has placed over their lives. Medical science says that numbness can be caused by an injured nerve. As an individual moves closer to becoming superficial often they find that the messages that inspired them before are now getting on their nerves. When the pastor shares about faithfulness, giving (especially if it's a pledge), or simply answering the call of God, superficial believers are likely to find those words to be an irritant. I suggest they're suffering from some nerve damage and it's causing spiritual numbness. They haven't lost all feeling yet but if no attention is given to their condition they could be well on their way.

Throughout the years as I've worked in ministry people have often talked about those who have their ears tickled by teaching that appeals to their personal desires more so than the desires God has for their lives. I liken that to the tingling sensation that is said to be a symptom of numbness. It's those things that initially don't hurt, but they do get our attention. If we're no longer accountable to leadership and it goes unchecked that tingling will ultimately cause much pain. There are many people who believe the church to be a detriment to their faith and therefore choose to serve God their own way. They help move more and more believers toward being superficial. The truth is that in the Old Testament God chose to pour His Spirit into the prophets. In the New Testament, God chose to pour His Spirit into His Son Jesus. Jesus spent His ministry pouring His life into His disciples so that they in turn, through the same Spirit would give birth to the church which is the vehicle through which God chooses to pour out His Spirit today. God established three great institutions in the world, first the family (Genesis 1:26-2:25), second government (The Pentateuch or Torah), and thirdly the church. (Acts 2; Colossians 1:18) The church may be flawed just like the people who oversee it and attend but it is nevertheless the vessel through which God chooses to pour out His Spirit upon the world. If you're starting to get the tingling sensation or tickling of your ears with the kind of deception that leads you away from the church, be very careful of the path you're on. Hebrews 10:24-25 says, "And let us consider one another in order to stir up good works, not forsaking the assembling of ourselves together, as is the manner of some, but exhorting one another, and so much the more as you see the Day approaching."

.

Decreased Blood-Flow

Another thing mentioned that could bring about numbness is a decrease in blood flow. I could preach on this all day long! Where would we be without the blood of Jesus flowing through our lives? Colossians 1:18 says, "And He is the head of the body, the church," and as I stated before, I believe Jesus is also the heart of the body because the heart is the muscle that pumps blood throughout the entire body. The bible says that the life is in the blood. (Genesis 9:4; Leviticus 17:11) Any limb on the body that

46

has a decrease in blood flow will begin to experience numbness. As any member of the body of Christ starts losing touch with the blood of Jesus their senses will grow dull in a number of areas. Without the blood covering our lives we become more susceptible to the enemies attacks. Remember it was the blood that caused Israel to be passed over during the tenth and final plague in Exodus 11-12, the death of the firstborn. It's the blood that cleanses us! Isaiah 1:18 says, "Though your sins are like scarlet, they shall be white as snow; though they be red like crimson, they shall be as wool." What a miracle working God we serve! God says my sins are red like scarlet and crimson, and the blood is red also. Only God could take red blood, apply it to red sin, and make it come out white! There is power in the blood! And any Christian who is suffering from a decrease in blood flow is in some serious trouble. It's no wonder that they would become superficial and display the characteristics of a prosthetic.

A decrease in blood flow is also an indication of broken fellowship with the Lord. One of the great sacraments in the church is communion which in many cases is conducted monthly. It's a time in which we have an opportunity to re-affirm our commitment to fellowship with Christ through His body and blood. In I Corinthians 11:27-29 there is a stern warning against having a superficial attitude when participating in communion. The word of God makes it clear that danger awaits the person who suffers from a decrease in blood flow. Ephesians 2:13 sys, "But now in Christ Jesus you who were once far off have been brought near by the blood of Christ." His blood draws us closer to Him! I would recommend that you and I make sure the blood has been applied to the doorposts and lintels of our house! He that has ears to hear, let him hear what the Spirit is saying!

Superficial Love

"My little children, let us not love in word or
in tongue, but in deed and in truth."
I John 3:18

When speaking of the end times Jesus said in Matthew 24:11-12, "Then many false prophets will rise up and deceive many. And because lawlessness will abound, the love of many will grow cold." Anyone who has been married for a number of years (personally I've been married for over 30 years) realizes that if a love relationship isn't nurtured and cared for there is a danger of that love growing cold or becoming superficial. If that holds true with our marriages how much more is it a truth that must be applied to our relationship with Christ? The bible teaches that our marriages are a reflection of the bond between Christ and the church. One thing that can't be debated is that no one wants their spouse to give them superficial love. But if we aren't careful, over time our love can start to grow cold. I find it interesting that Jesus says that "because lawlessness will abound the love of many will grow cold." That tells me God's people will be influenced by an ungodly society. The lawless behavior in the world will ultimately be mimicked by those who proclaim to be part of the church.

Isn't that what we're seeing today? The patterns of behavior we're constantly exposed to through television and various other media outlets are finding their way into the church. True love these days seems to be more of a fairy tale than something that's achievable. We must bring God our true love, not a superficial love. The bible teaches in two ways, explicitly or what's spoken plainly as in "You shall not steal" Exodus 20:15, and implicitly, something that's implied without necessarily being plainly stated, as in the Book of Acts which does not include the word "love" but the idea of love is implied throughout. The Book of Esther doesn't mention God, and yet He's found in it. The fact that God isn't interested in superficial love is taught all through the scriptures. With that in mind it's important that our love for God and His people be genuine.

Since the fall of man in the Garden of Eden (Genesis 3) the enemy has worked to keep us distanced from God. The devil sold Adam and Eve a bill of goods convincing them that eating from the Tree of the Knowledge of Good and Evil would improve them. Instead of the progress the devil suggested, they in fact regressed and their relationship with God suffered. In tasting the fruit they lost their innocence and total dependence on God, and were guilty of sin and now capable of operating independent from God. I've heard people these days refer to themselves as being "awoke" in reference to being open to multiple ways of thinking. The only thing that was awakened was sin. Interestingly, there was a Tree of Life in the Garden also, to which they were banned after eating from the forbidden tree. I guess when you get right down to it we always have a choice but too often for some the choice is poisonous. When one begins to live independent from God eternal life is no longer attainable. The independence Adam and Eve acquired that dreadful day has been a snare and a curse upon humanity ever since. One could argue that it is the culprit behind the superficial love we sometimes display. By opening their ears to the voice of Satan, Adam and Eve fell from grace. I recommend that you and I be very careful who we're listening to these days. Be sure that the voices you hear are fanning the flames of your love for God and not quenching the fire of your passion and enthusiasm.

Why do some people have the inclination to give a superficial love to the relationships that matter most to them? I'm certain there are a host of answers to that question, and I certainly won't pretend to have all of them, but I will on the basis of my experience and observation offer a few. Because of the effort required to keep a relationship healthy and thriving I believe some people feel it's too much work. Often our love for God becomes superficial as a result of complacency and/or laziness in spiritual matters. The time we give to building our relationship with the Lord must be born out of gratitude and a genuine love. There is a distinct difference between spending time with God and investing time with God. Spending time in a relationship can sometimes carry the idea of labor with no promise of reciprocation. On the other hand investing time in a relationship carries with it the idea of a definite return for any effort put forth. So you and I can spend time in prayer and run the risk of developing a superficial attitude because of the uncertainty of how effective we've been. Or we can invest time in prayer and come away refreshed and full of faith because we're confident that we have sown good seed into the relationship and therefore expect a return in the form of answers.

Secondly, it can also be the result of a lack of faith in the person they have a relationship with. I suggest that if a person doesn't invest quality time into their relationship with God, they're not likely to be familiar with His character. Typically when we're unfamiliar with the character of an individual, it's not uncommon for there to be a lack of trust. The sad truth is that even in some marriages, since there hasn't been quality investment from both parties involved, superficial love exists because they don't know each other well enough to give their full trust to the relationship. We give our full faith and trust to those we know intimately. It's imperative that we get to know God intimately in order that we can give Him our full faith and trust. The level of our faith can move us from superficial love to beneficial love.

The idea of getting to know God intimately is important to understanding that he can be trusted to be faithful in every area of our lives. Throughout the scripture we find the mighty acts of God being repeated in the hearing of His people in an effort to remind them of how faithful He's been. Moses reminded Israel of God's promise to Abraham and the fulfillment of that promise in their deliverance from Egypt. Joshua also reminded Israel of God's faithfulness. (Joshua 24) Many others in the Old Testament did the same. In the New Testament Israel was reminded of God's faithfulness by the Apostle Peter, by Stephen the Martyr, and by the Apostle Paul just to name a few. In every situation the purpose was to declare that God can be trusted. That if He did it before, He can do it again! If we recall the mighty acts of the

Lord in our own lives perhaps it would ward off that inclination to be superficial in our relationship with Him.

We know what Jesus says about those who are superficial, or the word He used to describe that attitude is, "lukewarm". Revelation 3:15-16 says, "I know your works, that you are neither cold nor hot. I could wish that you were cold or hot. So then, because you are lukewarm, and neither cold nor hot. I will vomit you out of My mouth." So it would seem that Jesus takes no pleasure in superficial love. That word "lukewarm" sufficiently describes a love that is superficial. When Jesus makes the statement that He'd rather we be cold or hot, He's saying that we're better off not being in relationship with Him at all, than to be half-hearted in our approach. I believe most of us would concur, it's better to have no love than to have a love that's superficial.

In addition to everything that's already been said there should also be an emphasis on giving the kind of love we expect to receive. If we're being completely honest we all want the very best from God, while often not giving Him our very best. I'm reminded of the words of the Apostle Paul in Galatians 6:7, "Do not be deceived, God is not mocked; for whatever a man sows, that he will also reap." I'm aware that this verse is most often quoted in reference to our giving, but it reflects a principle that is applicable in several areas our lives. To put it plainly, if you sow sparingly into your relationship with Christ, you shouldn't expect the fullness of His love outpoured into your life. Don't get me wrong, I'm not suggesting that God won't move in our lives at all, I'm simply saying that according to the principle taught in scripture, we receive based on the way we give whether that's money, love, or time, etc. it works the same way.

I'm trying to invest wholeheartedly into my relationship with God so I can reasonably expect His fullness in return. Otherwise I run the risk of setting myself up for disappointment. If we're giving the Lord a superficial love we shouldn't have an unrealistic expectation of what we'll receive in return. If you're like me and recognize that you'd be utterly and hopelessly lost without Jesus, then you also know how desperately we need Him every day of our lives. With that being said, how could we dare enter into His presence with anything less than our total devotion? For I delight in the law of God according to the inward man (Romans 7:22) but my flesh doesn't agree with my spirit. Like the words of the Psalmist (73:26) "My flesh and my heart fail; but God is the strength of my heart and my portion forever." I beseech you by the mercies of God, don't get trapped in the state of superficiality! If you've regressed and become superficial, get back on track

and make progress toward being beneficial.
I guarantee you won't regret it!

Chapter Three
"Being Artificial"
Cosmetic and Aesthetic

"Now as they were eating, He said, 'Assuredly, I say to you, one of you will betray Me.' And they were exceedingly sorrowful, and each of them began to say to Him, 'Lord, is it I?'" Matthew 26:21-22

Without a doubt brothers and sisters we have reached the stage in which the Prosthetic Parishioner is fully manifested. When a believer falls from the state of being a genuinely beneficial part of the body, to the state of being a superficial part of the body, they're in danger of becoming an artificial part of the body. A prosthetic if you will. For some the characterization of being artificial will sound very judgmental and therefore they won't be able to receive this prophetic warning from God. I would like to mention that I'm not trying to insinuate that I can distinguish the artificial from the genuinely beneficial. That ability belongs to the Lord Himself! I use the term "genuinely beneficial" because those who are artificial can still in some cases be beneficial. To be quite honest I'm too busy occupying myself with the business of insuring that I myself am not artificial to expend my energy on evaluating others. My hope and prayer is that this book will inspire you to evaluate yourself.

In the passage of scripture that opened this chapter we find Jesus speaking prophetically about His betrayer. Anyone who is even moderately familiar with the bible probably knows He was referring to Judas Iscariot. The setting is the last supper. Those in attendance are Jesus and the twelve disciples. A solemn and peaceful time of fellowship is interrupted by the startling announcement that He (Jesus) would be betrayed by one of the twelve. I find what happens next to be quite interesting, especially as I consider how I might have reacted had I been a part of that group of men. The bible says in verse 22 "each of them began to say to Him, 'Lord is it I?'" I'm amazed at the humility of the disciples. It appears that each one of them was willing to consider that they could possibly be guilty of the betrayal. We of course are privy to information the disciples didn't have which makes it easy for us to think they should have known it was Judas. But the truth is based on what they had seen from Judas they had no reason to suspect him. He had arrived at an artificial state in his relationship with the Lord but only Jesus and Judas were aware of it. Most often the artificial believer is known only by God and himself.

I would like to get back to the other eleven who said "Is is I?" Maybe it's just me but I'm surprised there wasn't an attitude in the room that said, "I bet I know who it is!" or "I always thought that brother was a little suspicious!" But instead the thought that prevailed was "Is it I?" It seems that everyone was thinking "I hope I'm not artificial!" These men, at least in that moment, had put aside their pride and arrogance, and considered themselves as the sinful beings we all are. The potential to fail in the area of sincerity and genuineness exists in all of us. It is only through a constant experience with God and with the indwelling power of the Holy Spirit that we can keep our hearts pure before the Lord. I can't help but wonder if someone will read this and say "That could never happen to me!" or will we be humble enough to pray "God please don't ever let that happen to me!"

Let's examine what it means to be artificial. I said earlier that even though something is artificial that doesn't mean it can't be beneficial and here's why. In order to make this point we'll consider artificial products and their purpose. For the sake of argument let's look at the Cubic Zirconia.

Many people own these stones because of their close resemblance to diamonds. In fact, only a trained eye could distinguish the difference between the Cubic Zirconia and a real or genuine diamond. It benefits the owner both cosmetically and aesthetically. Cosmetically, because it looks good to the person who owns it. And aesthetically, because it looks good to the person observing it. That's also the value of the prosthetic limb. It has a cosmetic quality because it gives the individual wearing it confidence in their appearance. It also has an aesthetic quality because it helps eliminate any awkwardness from others. Our minds are trained to see two arms, two legs, hands, feet, etc. There can sometimes be awkwardness when we meet someone with a missing limb. The prosthetic limb gives aesthetic balance to what we observe and puts people at ease. But again, just because their artificial doesn't mean they're not beneficial.

What about artificial sweeteners? For many people they turn out to be more beneficial than real sugar. These products such as Splenda, Equal, and several others are helpful to those with health concerns such as diabetes, or simply wanting to lose weight. Also there's artificial food coloring that's probably used more than most of us realize. So many of the food and drinks we consume have been given a more aesthetically pleasing color to grab our attention. So while the color may not be real it is still beneficial to those who manufacture it. My point is simply this: **The Prosthetic Parishioner** is capable of being of some value in the church which makes them very difficult to identify.

Making a U-Turn

What made it so difficult for the disciples to know that Judas was the betrayer? Let's look at it this way. If you're a licensed driver you have probably on some occasion had to follow someone to a destination. Because cars are equipped with turn signals and brake lights we're able to follow another vehicle with relative ease. For instance I know when I see the brake-lights come on we're preparing to stop. If I see the left turn signal I know we're either changing lanes or turning left depending on where we are on the road. A right turn signal does exactly the same only on the opposite side. But there is one thing the driver in front of me can do and there's no way for them to signal me that it's about to happen. And that is the u-turn! A u-turn can only be detected when it actually happens. The signal looks identical to the signal for a left turn. Only when the vehicle continues to turn until it's facing the opposite direction does it become clear what's happening.

In a similar way the disciples didn't see any signal that suggested Judas was about to make a u-turn. Only the trained eye of the Lord could see it coming. Judas had become artificial but because he maintained certain behaviors and habits in the presence of his brothers he appeared to be the same as the other disciples. He still functioned but not with the complete range of motion available to a genuinely beneficial believer. This is what makes the artificial stage so dangerous because one can get stuck and go unnoticed by others but never by God. How many of our brothers and sisters have left us in shock when they made an unexpected u-turn. We're often left saying "I never would have thought that could happen to him/her" That's because an artificial believer can still be beneficial in certain areas to maintain cosmetically and aesthetically.

Loss of Feeling

The artificial believer or **Prosthetic Parishioner** is susceptible to a loss of feeling with regard to the things of God. As I said earlier, in connection to the superficial believer, there is a decreased blood flow that results in spiritual numbness. However with the artificial believer there is often no blood flow at all. Much like the prosthetic limb, the only place where feeling exists is to the flesh it's connected to. The person who wears a prosthetic has feeling at the point of contact, not in the limb itself. In other words they are only moved or interested in the things that serve their own needs. It's in this place where an individual can cease to live their lives under the blood and begin relying on their own intellect and/or talents. Lines get blurred and it becomes increasingly difficult to distinguish God's voice from their own. It's also here where they no longer receive conviction from the preaching of God's word but interpret it as an attempt by the preacher to put them on a "guilt trip." This is one of the reasons the prosthetic often times cannot be reached or inspired to function in ministry.

The bible says in Leviticus 17:11, "For the life of the flesh is in the blood," which simply means that no part of the body can function without the blood. The word of God also teaches us that the blood of Jesus was shed at the cross of Calvary to atone for our sins. If we lose sight of the purpose and power of the blood we're in danger of devaluing not only what Christ done, but why He did it! If you have arrived at a place where you've lost feeling, the possibility exists that you are out of touch with the blood and therefore in an artificial state. We need to be reminded like the classic Andre Crouch song says, "The blood that gives me strength from day to day, it will never lose its power."

The Lesson of the Fig Tree

There are several places in Scripture where the fig tree is mentioned. I would like to recall just a few of them. The first record in the bible of the fig tree occurs in Genesis 3:7 where it's said that Adam and Eve "sewed fig leaves together and made themselves coverings." Also in Luke 19:4 a man named Zacchaeus is said to have climbed what most translations refer to as a "sycamore" tree. However if you exegete the word "sycamore" you'll find that the Greek word *"sukomoraia soo-kom-o-rah-yah or sukon soo-kon"* can also be translated as the word "fig". So for the sake of argument let's say Zacchaeus climbed a fig tree to see Jesus as He passed through Jericho. My point is that in both cases the fig tree is being used to cover up something. Adam and Eve were looking to cover themselves from being seen for what they had become (sinners) as a result of eating from the forbidden tree. One could also say that Zacchaeus being a sinner was using the fig tree for a covering as well. He probably thought the fig leaves would prevent Jesus from seeing him. Thankfully in both cases sin didn't prevent God from reaching out to them and it won't keep Him from reaching to you and me either. Oh and by the way, the hiding behind fig leaves thing didn't work. The trained eye of God saw right through them.

Let's turn our attention to a much more familiar passage, regarding the "cursing of the fig tree". It's found in three of the four gospels (excluding John), I'd like to use the record found in Mark's gospel. The verses I'd like to discuss are Mark 11:12-14; also verses 20-21. It reads like this:

"Now the next day, when they had come from Bethany, He was hungry. And seeing from afar a fig tree having leaves, He went to see if perhaps He would find something on it. When He came to it, He found nothing but leaves, for it was not the season for figs. In response Jesus said to it, 'Let no one eat fruit from you ever again.' And His disciples heard it." 11:12-14

"Now in the morning, as they passed by, they saw the fig tree dried up from the roots. And Peter, remembering, said to Him, "Rabbi, look! The fig tree which You cursed has withered away." 11:20-21

Obviously there is much that can be said about this incident in the life and ministry of Jesus and I don't presume to be able to explain it all. But I do intend to explain what the Spirit of God has revealed to me as it relates to this subject matter. The fact that Jesus was hungry I find very interesting. Not that He was hungry, because as a man there's nothing unusual about that. I mean interesting in the sense that it is included in the story. It also says that it wasn't the season for figs. So Jesus, being God, certainly would've known this which makes it so strange that He went to see if the tree had fruit. He is the creator of all things! So it's inconceivable that this fact would've escaped Him. So with that being said, this had to have been a teaching moment.

I'm under no illusion thinking that everyone will agree with the interpretation God has given me, but that doesn't discourage me from sharing what I believe is a prophetic word from the Lord. There is a clear eschatological message here and it's important that we don't miss it. The fig tree having leaves is a picture of the Christian having the appearance of fruitfulness. The leaves are what serve as the cosmetic covering. The aesthetic point is made when it says the fig tree with its leaves, were seen from afar and looked fruitful. The hunger mentioned relates to the worlds need to be fed the word of God by God's people. Christ's arrival at the fig tree is symbolic of His second coming when the church will be judged for its works. The fact that it wasn't the season for figs speaks to the truth that no one knows the day or the hour of His return. So we must be ready in season and out of season! I feel like preachin' right here!

So the fig tree, like the **Prosthetic Parishioner** was in fact artificial. It was properly arrayed in order to send the message of fruitfulness. For all intents and purposes it appeared to be right and proper. However, a close examination revealed the truth. The tree had some usefulness but it wasn't functioning fully the way it was created to. It was able to give shade but not fruit. If this had been an Oak tree or a Maple tree, giving shade may have been enough. But the fruit tree was created to give shade and fruit. It's not enough to just help people feel good, they must also be nourished and sustained by the word of God. The artificial believer can give shade but not fruit. But Jesus clearly commanded us to go and bear fruit. Many people today are coming to the church hungry. They see the leaves from afar but will they find fruit on the tree? The church looks aesthetically pleasing. But it's possible that the fruitfulness is only cosmetic. Those who have become artificial aren't only sitting in the pews or among the congregation they're also behind the pulpits. If you and I are in an artificial state we must do everything possible to get back to being genuinely beneficial. You may think it's not the season for Christ's return! Don't' be deceived no man knows the day or the hour! Jesus said watch!

This is a very sobering truth for those who might be trapped in an artificial state. It speaks to our need to be ready for Christ's return! But there is good news for anyone who's struggling to get back to a place of productivity and that is God is in the business of doing the miraculous through His grace. While the previous passage concerning the fig tree speaks of God's judgment, I would like to examine a parable about the fig tree that speaks of His grace. It's found in the gospel of Luke 13:6-9. It reads like this:

"He also spoke this parable: 'A certain man had a fig tree planted in his vineyard, and he came seeking fruit and found none. Then he said to the keeper of his vineyard, "Look, for three years I have come seeking fruit on this fig tree and found none. Cut it down, why does it use up the ground?" But he answered and said to him, "Sir, let it alone this year also, until I dig around it and fertilize it, and if it bears fruit, well. But if not, after that you can cut it down"'

I'm so glad that He is the God of another chance! There are some similarities between this fig tree and the one previously discussed. The biggest difference is in how the story ends. The picture is given of the owner of a vineyard with an unproductive fig tree. In fact it has failed to produce for three years and in each of those years the owner has been disappointed to discover the tree has not yielded any figs. Much like the illustration involving Jesus, the tree looked good but as we know looks can be deceiving. Another difference is that the owner would've been arriving during the season for figs otherwise it makes no sense that he expected to find them. It was this fact that fueled his anger and caused him to suggest that the tree be cut down. He went as far as to claim the ground would be better served without the fig tree. He said, "why does it use up the ground?" But the workers willingness to try one more time by digging around the tree and fertilizing it saved the tree.

I wonder how many of us can relate to that fig tree? There are times when we all fail to live up to the standard God has set for our lives. As painful as it may be to admit, some have been repeat offenders. The three consecutive years speak to the fact that it isn't just baby Christians, but more mature Christians who fail to live and function productively. But thanks be to God that He never gives up on us! You may be reading this book and feeling like a failure in the eyes of God but let me encourage you and remind you that He's willing to do some digging and some fertilizing to help restore you. For sure no one knows the hour of Christ's return which makes it incumbent upon us to take advantage of the opportunity to get back to the place of being a fully functional, beneficial part of the body! God will use your Pastor's or perhaps other leadership in the church to do a little digging and fertilizing to help you become fruitful again. It is the will of God that we be fruitful as Christians. (John 15:1-8) I believe the Spirit of God is warning the church when the worker says, "let it alone this year also... And if it bears fruit, well. But if not, after that you can cut it down." For some the Spirit is saying this could be your last chance to respond to the love of God. Is this that one more year for you? I believe you and I must take that into consideration if we're living in an artificial state.

Just like the fig tree in the first illustration there were leaves that contributed to its cosmetic appearance. And because it looked good aesthetically the owner of the vineyard for three years had an expectation to receive fruit from the tree. Much like in this parable there are people who come year after year into our churches expecting to find fruit. Most parishioners, especially those in leadership, are aesthetically pleasing but that begs the question, is it just cosmetic or is it authentic? Like a jeweler with a trained eye to distinguish the difference between a cubic zirconia and a real diamond, God has the trained eye to differentiate between the two. The cubic zirconia can fulfill all the functions of a real diamond except it doesn't cut glass. The **Prosthetic Parishioner** can fulfill most of the functions of a genuinely beneficial believer except he lacks the cutting edge that belongs to those whose heart is right with God. Because the blood isn't flowing through their lives they have no feeling and therefore cannot be sensitive to the moving of the Holy Spirit.

In Numbers 15:30-31 the bible speaks of the consequences of presumptuous sin. This particular sin can only be committed by a believer. To presume God's forgiveness prior to committing a sin is a serious offense to God. In fact the bible says that person shall be "cut off" or amputated if you will. The problem with being "cut off" is that most people are unaware when it happens and attempt to function as though they're still connected to the body as they were prior to their sin. They will usually discover their condition much like Samson did in Judges 16:20. Samson said, "I will go out as before, at other times, and shake myself free!" But he did not know that the Lord had departed from him. I wonder how many Christians have regressed to an artificial state and become ignorant of the fact that they've lost their cutting edge? The sin of Samson was a presumptuous one to be sure and he was unknowingly cut off from God's indwelling power. The bottom line is that sin is what causes a believer to regress to the place of being artificial. How tragic that one would arrive at a place where because of sin they've been rendered powerless but be unaware. The man of God, much like Samson, should not give place to the devil and then assume to access God's power upon demand.

There is good news for the **Prosthetic Parishioner** and it's simply this, God is in the business of restoration. He is the God of another chance! Even after Samson's pride, arrogance, and lust, caused him to fail God the bible says in Judges 16:22, "However, the hair of his head began to grow again after it had been shaven." Although he had become artificial as a result of his sin, God didn't give up on him and he won't give up on you either! There is hope for those who have fallen from where they once were spiritually and lost their genuineness. It doesn't matter if your love has become artificial. Or perhaps your commitment or your walk has become artificial. God can still lead you on a path toward becoming beneficial again. All it takes is a willingness to humble ourselves under the mighty hand of God and surrender everything to Him all over again. In this next chapter we'll talk about what it takes to go from an artificial part of the body back to being a genuinely beneficial part of the body.

Chapter Four
Being Sacrificial
"A Life Poured Out"

"I beseech you therefore, brethren, by the mercies of God, that you present your bodies a living sacrifice, holy, acceptable to God, which is your reasonable service. And do not be conformed to this world, but be transformed by the renewing of your mind, that you may prove what is that good and acceptable and perfect will of God." Romans 12:1-2

The road to regression that starts at being beneficial, then superficial, then artificial can be reversed by living sacrificial. It's not possible to be a beneficial part of the body without living sacrificial. Once a believer gives in to that superficial spirit, sacrificial living goes right out the window! The scripture says a "living sacrifice" which means, (You guessed it!) living sacrificial. If we consider the function of our bodies we can see that sacrificial behavior is part of our nature. For instance, let's consider a situation in which the threat of bodily harm exists. Rather than allowing my head to suffer injury my hands or arms would instinctively move into a protective position thereby sacrificing themselves for the more vital part of the body. If we take that thought a step further we can also consider the fetal position we're taught to assume for protection from an attack. In doing so, we sacrifice damage to our arms and legs to protect the more vital parts of our bodies, like our head and chest. So there is a natural Inclination for the body to sacrifice. If the church body were so inclined to sacrifice for one another we would witness an amazing demonstration of God's love. We would be more protective of our brothers and sisters, and especially our leaders. In a similar way to how the natural body sacrifice's to protects itself, the spiritual body of Christ must sacrifice for each other as well.

Jesus says in John 15:13, "Greater love has no one than this, than to lay down one's life for his friends." This verse speaks of the ultimate demonstration of human love. The willingness to sacrifice for one another is a true testament to the love of God living in and through us. Jesus took His love and sacrifice to another level when the scripture says in Romans 5:8, "But God demonstrates His own love toward us, in that while we were still sinners, Christ died for us." So Jesus not only laid down His life for His friends, but for His enemies also. That's divine love! It's not outside the realm of possibility to imagine someone having a John 15:13 kind of love. But to see a Romans 5:8 kind of love it takes divine intervention. Only Jesus could do that, and I for one am very grateful!

I'd be remiss if I didn't mention that in Romans 12:1 when the Apostle Paul says a "living sacrifice" his intention was to be a contrast from that of the dead animal sacrifices that were common during those times. It speaks to the fact that God isn't interested in a dead sacrifice but He's looking for a life that is lived sacrificially to bring Him glory. Jesus lived and gave His life as a "living sacrifice" and exemplified the type of lifestyle we should all strive for. His selfless love and total commitment to His father's will is the model for us to follow. I believe the sacrificial life invites the blessing and favor of God upon us and leads to the kind of success He truly desires for us to experience. It would be foolish to dismiss the idea of sacrifice because of its difficulty without testing the veracity of its rewards.

Taking One for the Team

Anyone who knows me well also knows that I'm a huge sports fan. Many people all over the world enjoy the competitive and unpredictable nature of sports. For me, that's all the reality television I need. I want to examine the sacrificial element involved in team sports. It's in team sports where I believe some of the greatest life lessons are learned. Also for the most part every ministry leader is involved in team building in order to effectively grow his ministry and have the greatest impact on the kingdom of God. We've heard many of the clichés like, "It takes Teamwork to make the Dream work." There is also the acronym T.E.A.M. (Together Everyone Accomplishes More) the truth is that the team concept is only successful when sacrifice is applied to the mission.

The team sports I'm most fond of are Baseball, Football, and Basketball, and each of them require sacrifice by its team members to achieve the highest level of success. In Baseball there is what's called the sacrifice fly as well as the sacrifice bunt. Both plays involve the batter making an out to advance the base runner. If a runner is on third base with less than two outs a batter can hit a deep (sacrifice) fly ball allowing the runner at third to tag and score on the out. It can also be used to advance a runner into scoring position. Even though the batter makes an out he/she will be celebrated by their teammates for sacrificing themselves for the good of the team. Many times a good hitter may be asked by their manager to lay down a sacrifice bunt to advance a runner into scoring position. Once again the batter is out but the team has been helped by the sacrifice.

In Football and Basketball the sacrifices are less obvious but no less effective. In Football the skill position players (Quarterbacks, Running Backs, & Receivers) generally get all of the recognition for the team's accomplishments, however it's the rarely recognized players who are largely responsible for their achievements. On every successful play there are obscure players making blocks that ensure everything goes as planned. If no one sacrifices their bodies to block the Quarterback doesn't have time to throw to his receivers, nor does the running back have holes to run through and gain yardage on the plays. Teams only succeed when there's sacrifice!

Even in Basketball sacrifices are being made regularly to help players succeed. We all celebrate players like Michael Jordan, Kobe Bryant, or LeBron James, but those men understand the sacrifices of their teammates. We see the beauty of the shot going in the basket and oftentimes miss the player who sacrificed to pick off a defender who could have possibly blocked the shot. All throughout the game there are players sacrificing their bodies for sake of the team. Most of the time they're recognized and celebrated by their teammates but not the public, but they understand that even though one person gets most of the credit it's a win for everyone.

The point I'm trying to make is that we must belong to the body or team in order for our sacrifice to make the greatest impact for the kingdom of God. In the world of sports many unknown or obscure players have enjoyed lengthy careers because of their willingness to sacrifice. In the body of Christ the key to a long lasting relationship with God is found in our willingness to live sacrificially. It allows us to live out the words found in Philippians 2:3-4, "Let nothing be done through selfish ambition or conceit, but in lowliness of mind let each esteem others better than himself. Let each of you look out not only for his own interests, but also for the interests of others." We are most beneficial to the body when we are sacrificial for the body.

The Sacrifice God Desires

Hebrews 13:15-16 says, "Therefore by Him let us continually offer the sacrifice of praise to God, that is, the fruit of our lips, giving thanks to His name. But do not forget to do good and to share, for with such sacrifices God is well pleased." The idea of sacrifice is found all throughout scripture from Abraham being willing to offer his son Isaac (Genesis 22) to God the Father offering His son Jesus on the cross for the sins of the world. The prophet Jeremiah in chapter 17, verse 26, speaks of "bringing the sacrifices of praise to the house of the Lord." Clearly the sacrifice God desires is about action but it's also about attitude.

In the book of Leviticus chapter one, the Burnt Offering is described. It speaks about what should be sacrificed, how it should be sacrificed, and the atoning quality of the sacrifice. In verse three it says the offering should be of one's own free will, and that it should be without blemish, and that it should be male. It was unacceptable to offer an animal with any kind of defect. God was looking for the very best when it came time for sacrifice. There was also a requirement that it be done willingly. A sacrifice given grudgingly was incapable of pleasing God. The giving of a male was significant because they were necessary for reproductive purposes. Their seed was absolutely essential to procreate their species which made every male animal given, especially one without blemish, a sacrifice for those dependent upon the flock for food and business. In verse five we are told the animal is a bull, probably the most expensive animal to part with.

If that person either didn't possess or couldn't afford a bull they were to bring a sheep or a goat. In the same manner as the bull, they were to be male and without blemish, in other words the very best one could bring. If that person either didn't possess or couldn't afford a sheep or goat, they were to bring turtledoves or pigeons. The bottom line is that the sacrifice was to be the very best a person could offer from what he or she possessed.

Although the book of Leviticus is for many a very difficult book to read, there is much value to found in its content. I remember early in my walk with God I found reading Leviticus to be like reading my car contract. It wasn't high on my priority list for bible study. Over the years as I've grown and committed myself to reading the entire bible yearly, my perspective has changed. And while it does remain one of the more difficult books to read, I have nevertheless found great truth and insight in Leviticus. The things that appeared on the surface to be excessive and repetitious religious rules and rituals were actually shedding light on the holiness of God. The truth is the book of Leviticus enlightens us with its main message, which is holiness. It presents the case for mankind's need of a savior. All the various sacrifices described in Leviticus paint a picture of the righteous requirements of a holy God.

Every sacrifice in the law had as its purpose the design of drawing us to the conclusion of our need for Jesus Christ. In Galatians 3:24 the Apostle Paul says, "Therefore the law was our tutor to bring us to Christ, that we might be justified by faith." A Tutor is someone (or in this case something) charged with the instruction and guidance of another. So then the scripture teaches us that the law had a purpose, and that purpose was to instruct or guide us to Jesus Christ. It intended to lead us to the One who is the ultimate example of what it means to be a living sacrifice. It is His life that we are to emulate.

Even through the animal sacrifices seen in the Old Testament the message is clear,

"Give God your absolute best!" It is through living sacrificial that we must strive to bring an unblemished, healthy lifestyle before a holy God. That being said, we should all be eternally grateful that the Lord has continued to accept our far less than perfect sacrifice. All because of the grace of God being demonstrated in the person of Jesus Christ, by His life, death, and resurrection. I've come to realize that His grace by no means is an excuse for willful disobedience and rebellion against God but it does relieve us from guilt when we stumble as we so often do along the way.

The bible says in Romans 8:1-2, "There is therefore now no condemnation to those who are in Christ Jesus, who do not walk according to the flesh, but according to the Spirit. For the law of the Spirit of life in Christ Jesus has made me free from the law of sin and death." Here the Apostle Paul makes us aware of two laws we encounter as Christians. There is the law of the Spirit of life in Christ Jesus, and there is the law of sin and death. We are not condemned because the law of the Spirit of life in Christ Jesus is greater than the law of sin and death. When we give our lives to Jesus we come under the power and authority of the greater law. The law of the Spirit of life in Christ Jesus is the law under which we are saved. What then is the law of sin and death? I believe it is found in James 1:14-15 when the bible says, "But each one is tempted when he is drawn away by his own desires and enticed. Then when desire has conceived, it gives birth to sin; and sin, when it is full grown, brings forth death." I find the language in these verses very interesting. James uses the words conceived (or conception), birth, and full grown giving a vivid description of how progressively the law of sin and death affect the believer. The law of sin and death is the law in which those who walk according to the flesh are under. But I say again the law of the Spirit of life in Christ Jesus is greater than the law of sin and death, and therefore we are not condemned!

It is with that in mind that we are able to bring our flawed lives to God as a living sacrifice and be accepted. However, it is still imperative that we bring God the very best that we can offer Him as a sweet smelling aroma that He might be pleased. So if we are to avoid the pitfalls of going from being a fully functional, productive, beneficial part of the body, to becoming a superficial part, and even descending to an artificial part of the body, we must commit to living sacrificial. Living a life built on prayer and fasting. Also a life built on the reading and study of God's word. And perhaps the most important thing is living a life love for God and man as well as obedience to the will of God.

As a member of Victory Outreach International for the past 31 years, I've been constantly challenged to sacrifice for the sake of the vision God has given our ministry. We are truly a vision driven ministry thanks to our founders Pastor Sonny and Sister Julie Arguinzoni. Certainly our church is not for everyone. We are very active and busy in the inner-city and that isn't where everyone is comfortable. I spent eight years as a Senior Pastor in the inner-city in Washington DC and I can tell you from experience that it required much sacrifice. But the souls that were saved and the lives that were changed made every sacrifice well worth it! Whenever I've begun to drift or lose focus over the years it has been the emphasis on the vision that has helped me to re-align my life with God's will. Don't underestimate the value of being part of a body of believers with a God-given vision and a steadfast determination to see it fulfilled. Living a sacrificial life requires not only living a submitted life to God Himself, but submitting to Him through the leadership He places over us. That's where the real sacrificing happens when we allow

God's people to have the authority to speak into our lives correctively and directionally. It's sacrificing our will for His will!

Time is Everything

As I consider the value and necessity of living sacrificially I can't help but think of my most precious commodity. Some would think that equates to money but that's not it. Make no mistake, money is certainly a precious commodity and there absolutely needs to be sacrifice with our finances. Some would possibly suggest family to be their most precious commodity and without a doubt it is very high on the list. But at the end of the day it is time that is our most precious commodity. It amounts to that one thing in life that is irreplaceable. Even as I write this book I realize that these are moments in time that can never be recovered. As sure as the sun rises and sets each one of us are aging with each passing minute.

I've always found it interesting that we use similar language when discussing time as we do when discussing money. We speak of spending time as well as spending money. We often say we're saving time as well as saving money. Although we understand that saving time is a figure of speech because truthfully time cannot be saved. There is also the idea of wasting time and investing time both of which are things that can be done with finances. I'm at a place in my life where I'd like to focus on investing my time as opposed to simply spending it. Saving time is something I've given up on because I realize it's impossible. And if I'm completely honest I waste far more time than I should. Especially when I consider that I'm now 60 years old and entering the fourth quarter of life. I truly want to get the most out of whatever time I have left. The difference between spending and investing is that when I'm a spender I expect an immediate return, but when I'm an investor I patiently wait for the reward of my efforts.

Sacrificing my time for the glory of God means I need to discipline myself to do less spending of my time and resist the urge to waste time. During the years of my youthful indiscretions I wasted plenty of time being addicted to drugs and alcohol. But I've discovered that those aren't the only things in life that can be counterproductive and wasteful. There are several activities in which I can find myself wasting precious time that could be invested into the kingdom of God. Things like Television, Cell Phones, the Internet, and relationships that serve no purpose in our spiritual development or God-given assignment in life. One of the great benefits of serving God through being actively involved in the building of His church is that it allows me to invest my time. And I'm convinced that investment will bring a return not only in this life but in the one to come.

David the Psalmist declares in Psalm 27:13, "I would have lost heart, unless I had believed that I would see the goodness of the Lord in the land of the living." Clearly that time investment isn't only rewarded when we get to heaven but also for here during our time on earth. When we set aside selfishness and sacrifice our time and invest it into the lives of others there is a sure reward from God. Without question it can be very difficult to give our time and attention to others particularly when we have families. Our obligations to our wives and children shouldn't be neglected, but they also shouldn't be used as an excuse for not sowing our time and talents into the lives of others. The word of God says in Galatians 6:10, "Therefore, as we have opportunity, let us do good to all, especially those who are of the household of faith." I reference this particular verse because when it uses the word "therefore" it is related to previous verses about sowing and reaping. In verse 7 (which is appropriately used in connection with giving) it says "whatever a man sows, that he will also reap." Keep in mind that we give of our time, talent and treasure.

The bottom line is that living sacrificially involves a host of things and I wouldn't pretend to be able mention them all without leaving something unsaid. But be that as it may, I'm confident that my point has been made and that is sacrificial living will prevent superficial living and artificial living. It is the key to maintaining our lives as a beneficial part of the body of Christ. And when it's all said and done we should all strive to be a fully functional part of the body with a complete range of motion. We should have the blood of Jesus flowing through our lives so that we don't become numb and lose feeling as it relates to the things that move God's heart. It's easy to get trapped because superficial people and artificial people can still do some good. Those things can fool someone into believing it is okay to stay where they are. But we must remember that what is capable of fooling man is incapable of fooling God. Never be satisfied just being good! As followers of Christ we should always and every situation, strive for greatness!

Chapter Five
"The Last Words"

I truly feel that writing this book is an act of obedience to God for me. It's unnecessary for me to divulge intimate details about my personal life, but suffice it to say that I'm writing from experience. Anyone who's walked with God for a great number of years is aware that the Christian Life is full of ups and downs. If we pay attention to detail we can expect to have more ups than downs. As it has been said by many over the years, "There's no shame in getting knocked down as long as you don't stay down!" In this fight of faith all of us have taken some serious hits at times but being a person who is consistent in their spiritual disciplines (prayer, fasting, reading God's word) will build the resiliency one needs to bounce back!

Becoming or being a **Prosthetic Parishioner** isn't the end of all things for the believer. As I've stated throughout the book, falling from Beneficial, to Superficial, to Artificial, can be remedied by living Sacrificial. It's in the Sacrificial living that we can get back to being fully functional, productive Christians with a full range of motion. If you're starting to have spiritual numbness it could be that you're experiencing a decreased blood flow. Don't wait until there's a complete loss of feeling as a result of no blood flowing at all. Let every day of your life be an opportunity to love God with all your heart, soul, and strength!

Maybe you're one who says, "I'm struggling with some areas of sin in my life but I'm too ashamed to confess it." The love of God can set you free from guilt and shame! But you can still take the matter to God in prayer! Matthew 6:6 says, "But you, when you pray, go into your room, and when you have shut the door, pray to your Father who is in the secret place; and your

Father who sees in secret will reward you openly." I love the idea being conveyed here. I can go to my room, shut the door, and pray in secret! I call this my "none of your business praying!" The truth is we all have some things we need to pray about and it's best if it's only between us and God. There are certain things that belong only in the secret place. The good news is that Jesus says that our Father is in the secret place! But it gets even better than that! Our Father rewards openly the things prayed about secretly! Don't let the devil lie to you our God is rich in mercy and full of compassion.

So let's get back to being Beneficial parts of the body of Christ! Remember God chose you and gifted you to be an important part of the work He's doing in the world today! Don't dial back your level of commitment to God by diminishing your involvement in ministry, it's through the church that God's Spirit is being poured out! Whatever you do child of God live your life in such a way as to make the greatest impact for Christ you can possibly make before you leave this earth! Being a **Prosthetic Parishioner** is the charge many believers face today! The world is bringing an accusation against the people of God saying that we're either superficial or artificial. Present your body a living sacrifice holy, and acceptable to God! And prove what the will of God is for your life! So when your Christianity is on trial and you're accused of being a **Prosthetic Parishioner,** make every effort to be able to enter a plea of NOT GUILTY!

The Lesson of the Fallen Branch

When it comes to hearing God's voice it often happens in the most unlikely of circumstances. In my life it seems that God usually speaks to me when I'm least expecting to hear from Him. Experience has taught me that God speaks to me when He knows I'm ready, not when I think I'm ready. The honest truth is that there are many occasions when I'm wrestling in my spirit about the things I go through. I've been serving the Lord for over thirty years now and like most Christians I envisioned myself to have accomplished more in my life by this time. We must all be very careful during these seasons of our lives because it can lead to feeling dissatisfied with what God is doing. It's understandable to have an "I'm not satisfied, I want more!" attitude when it comes to fulfilling God's purpose for our lives but we shouldn't become unhappy in God's process. I believe that when we allow ourselves to yield to these types of thoughts, it can put us in an emotionally compromised state. I'm sure you've been there. It's the place where your feelings dictate your level of faith, rather than your faith dictating the level of your feelings. Whenever that happens, we can be guilty of sinning against God through our lack of trust in how He chooses to bring to fruition the promises He made to us in His word.

About two years ago I began battling with feelings of failure and insignificance. Not that I had done anything in particular to contribute to those feelings but it was the work of the devil to try and frustrate my purpose in Christ. As a husband and father I started to really feel the weight of my family's struggles. My ministry wasn't thriving the way I had hoped and as a result we were experiencing problems financially and I was having a hard time seeing God as Jehovah Jireh, my Provider! Fortunately I never allowed those emotions to affect my daily Bible reading schedule but I must confess it had an adverse effect on my prayer life. Even though I was faithfully attending church and remaining involved as a leader and minister in the local ministry where I'm currently planted. I served where I could, I tithed regularly with the limited amount of resources I had. I counseled with men and women in the church, I encouraged my wife while she struggled to find steady work, all the while I was fighting my own inner battles with my faith. I'm sure there are many others who've gone through similar situations. The word of God says in I Peter 3:12, "Beloved, do not think it strange concerning the fiery trial which is to try you, as though some strange thing happened to you;" We are all at some point facing the same kind of situations in our lives! The dilemma I faced was compounded by the fact that I believe when the Bible says that "the husband is the head of the wife" that it suggests that he is responsible for the state of his wife and his family. The devil used my own convictions to make me feel as though I wasn't measuring up. I guess the bottom line is that I was feeling disconnected from the Lord.

One day as I was walking home, and not particularly enthused about my condition at the time. I observed something that God spoke clearly and specifically to me through. I live in Palmdale, California which is located in the Antelope Valley. It's in the High Desert on the outskirts of the Mojave. For those who are familiar with the area, you've seen the many wide open spaces scattered with Joshua Trees and Tumble Weeds and not much else. On the street where I often walk on my way home there is an open space that fits that description. In fact, on the East side of the street the sidewalk is unpaved. On one occasion during the fall as I made my home I observed a City vehicle (Bulldozer) driving onto the dirt walkway with the purpose of clearing the walkway because of a tree that had grown out and was blocking the path. The driver used the front end, or blade to push the branch away from the walking path. The force of the vehicle pushing the branch caused it to break. I could hear the sound of wood cracking as the driver forced the branch over into the field. I remember thinking the result of this action would bring death to the branch because it appeared to have been severed from the tree. At the time there didn't seem to be anything unusual about what I had witnessed and so I just went about my business as I always had.

As the months went by I continued to walk along that same path on my way home seeing that fallen branch every time I passed it. Interestingly, or perhaps fortunately that year during the spring we got a decent amount of rain which for those of us living in Southern California, we were extremely grateful. Of course that resulted in flowers blooming, trees sprouting their green leaves. Basically God began to paint the High Desert with beautiful spring colors. As I passed the fallen branch one day something caught my attention that I had not anticipated. The fallen branch had begun to sprout brand new leaves. They were beautiful and green. They were as

vibrant and strong as the leaves on the
main part of the tree! The voice inside my
head was saying, "I thought this branch was
dead! How could it bear new growth some
two months after it was broken?" As it
turns out I thought the branch had been
completely detached from the tree but
what I couldn't see was that even though it
had been broken it was still connected to
the tree. While the connection wasn't as
strong as before it nevertheless still allowed
the branch to receive life from the tree! The
tree was still transferring what was
necessary for the branch to blossom and
bud even while it was lying parallel to the
ground. What I was able to discern was the
position of the branch and because of that I
pronounced a judgment of death to it.
What I was unable to discern was the
condition of the branch and because of that
I couldn't see that there was still hope, and
the potential for it to live and thrive again.
The only thing branch needed was a little
help!

It was in this setting that God began to speak to me about not only my life, but the lives of many others in Christianity. The tree and the fallen branch were a reflection of my life and relationship with Christ. The tree was a representation of Jesus and I was the fallen branch, broken by outside forces over which it had no control. John 15:5 says, "I am the vine, you are the branches. He who abides in Me, and I in him, bears much fruit; for without Me you can do nothing." The more I considered the fallen branch, the more I seen myself in it. I saw my pride and judgmental attitude toward others when they had fallen. I thought about all the people who because of their position I counted them out while not knowing their true condition. Many times I even felt somewhat awkward and uncomfortable dealing with them once they had bounced back. Our pride can lead to feelings of superiority, and that can expose some of the ugliness that resides in our hearts.

The prophet Jeremiah details the condition of our hearts in chapter 17 and verse 9 when he says, "The heart is deceitful above all things, and desperately wicked; who can know it?" Jeremiah diagnoses the sickness of man's heart while the prophet Ezekiel gives us the remedy for the hearts ailment. Ezekiel 11:19-20 says, "Then I will give them one heart, and I will put a new spirit within them, and take the stony heart out of their flesh, and give them a heart of flesh, that they may walk in My statutes and keep My judgments and do them; and they shall be My people, and I will be their God." While Jeremiah asks the rhetorical question "Who can know it?" (The heart) the obvious answer is God alone can know the heart of man. The prophet Ezekiel declares the heart to be beyond repair and therefore he suggests it must be replaced. He says that God must "take the stony heart out of their flesh, and give them a heart of flesh…" Maybe it's just me but that makes me question the times I've referred to someone as having a good heart. Especially when referring to an un-regenerated soul, or un-saved person. My point being that the fallen branch exposed some of the ugliness in my own heart.

The first thing I'd like to examine is getting knocked down. The way I see it the branch was doing fine until an unanticipated blow was delivered that resulted in its falling. That's the way it goes sometimes in this fight of faith. It's getting blindsided by things that hurt the most. It's similar to the sport of boxing. Fighters are generally hurt most by the punches they didn't see coming. Those are the blows that typically result in a knockout. When they're able to see a punch coming, they brace themselves and are less likely to get hurt as badly. I must confess that I've taken my fair share of unanticipated blows and on some occasions suffered a spiritual TKO! The good thing is someone was there to help me get back in the fight.

It's a sad truth but people who get knocked down aren't always offered a helping hand. Sometimes even Christians will join in with the world and condemn rather than encourage. If you've ever been counted out, you know what I'm talking about. Many people will find it easier to focus on your faults and not your faith. That's because a natural man can only see faults, he can't see faith! I Corinthians 2:14 says, "But the natural man does not receive the things of the Spirit of God, for they are foolishness to him; nor can he know them, because they are spiritually discerned." It takes someone filled with the Holy Spirit to look for the remnant of faith in those who have fallen. You see, the reality is that a fallen saint is still a saint! Being down doesn't necessarily equate to being disconnected! In Hebrews 13:5 He says, "I will never leave you nor forsake you." And that promise can be relied on even during those times when we've been knocked down! Just like with the fallen branch there remained a connection to the tree that wasn't visible to me but nevertheless was still capable of sending life into the branch.

At the end of the day the superficial or artificial believer shouldn't be counted out. They may have been blindsided by circumstances that left them weak and ineffective. But a Spirit filled Saint can help them get back to sacrificial living which will in turn lead them back to being beneficial. Through the power of the Holy Spirit even a Prosthetic can be changed!

119

Made in the USA
Las Vegas, NV
04 November 2023

80240071R00069